The Let's Talk Library™

Let's Talk About When You Have to Get Stitches

Melanie Ann Apel

The Rosen Publishing Group's
PowerKids Press™
New York

Published in 2002 by The Rosen Publishing Group, Inc.
29 East 21st Street, New York, NY 10010

First Edition

Book Design: Erin McKenna

Layout Design: Colin Dizengoff

Project Editors: Jennifer Landau, Jennifer Quasha, and Jason Moring

Photo Credits: pp. 4, 8, 11 © Photo Researchers; p. 7 © Telefocus; p. 12 © The Image Works; pp. 15, 19 © Kate Preftakes; p. 16 © Maura Boruchow; p. 20 © Custom Medical

Apel, Melanie Ann.
    Let's talk about when you have to get stitches / Melanie Ann Apel. — 1st ed.
        p. cm. —(The let's talk about library)
Includes index.
    ISBN 0-8239-5861-2
    1. Sutures—Juvenile literature. I. Title. II. Series.
RD73.S8 A64 2002
617'.9178—dc21
                                                                    00-012192

Manufactured in the United States of America

Contents

1 Tristan and Josh 5

2 What Are Stitches? 6

3 Why You Need Stitches 9

4 Scars 10

5 Getting Stitches 13

6 Feeling Scared 14

7 Reasons People Get Stitches 17

8 Taking Care of Your Stitches 18

9 Getting Stitches Taken Out 21

10 Getting Help When You Need Stitches 22

   Glossary 23

   Index 24

Tristan and Josh

Tristan and Josh like to play outside. They have a lot of fun together. They are always careful when they play. Today Josh fell off his bike and cut his knee. The cut was deep. It would not stop bleeding. Josh had to go to the hospital. He had to get **stitches** to close the cut on his knee.

◀ *Bike accidents can cause injuries that require stitches.*

5

What Are Stitches?

Have you ever seen someone thread a needle and sew a piece of fabric? The needle is passed in and out of the fabric. The thread left in the fabric makes stitches. When someone has a cut that will not close on its own, the cut needs stitches. The cut is sewn with a needle and thread just like the fabric.

Special hospital needles and thread are used on the stitches we get, but the stitches we get are similar to those sewn into fabric. ▶

Why You Need Stitches

When you cut yourself, your body has a special way of mending the cut. This is called healing. If the cut is very deep, it may take a long time to heal on its own. A cut that stays open for too long can get **infected**. Stitches close the cut so it can heal faster. Stitches also will help keep dirt from getting inside the cut and infecting it.

◀ *Cuts need to be covered so that sand and dirt do not get into them.*

Scars

A **scar** is a mark left on your skin after a cut has healed completely. Some cuts don't leave a scar. Other cuts, especially big or deep ones, leave scars. A cut that needs stitches usually will leave a scar. Stitches pull your skin tightly together. Stitches actually make sure that the scar is smaller than it would be without them.

*The chin is a common place ▶
to have a scar.*

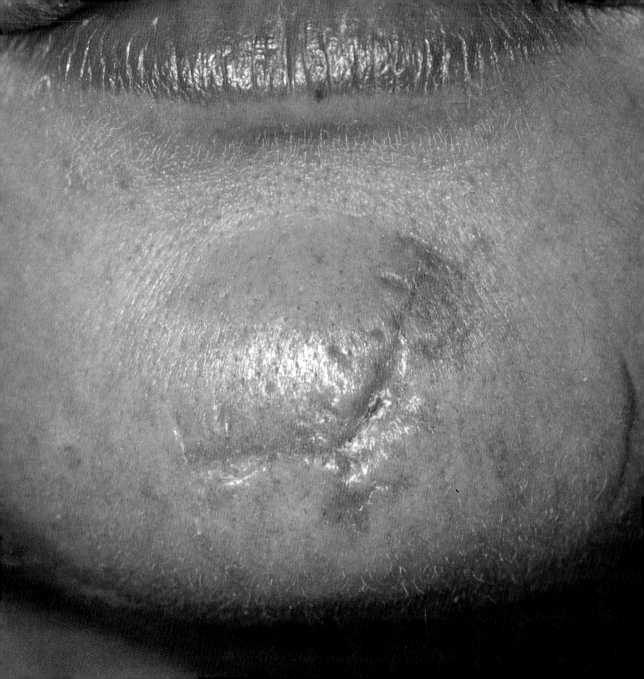

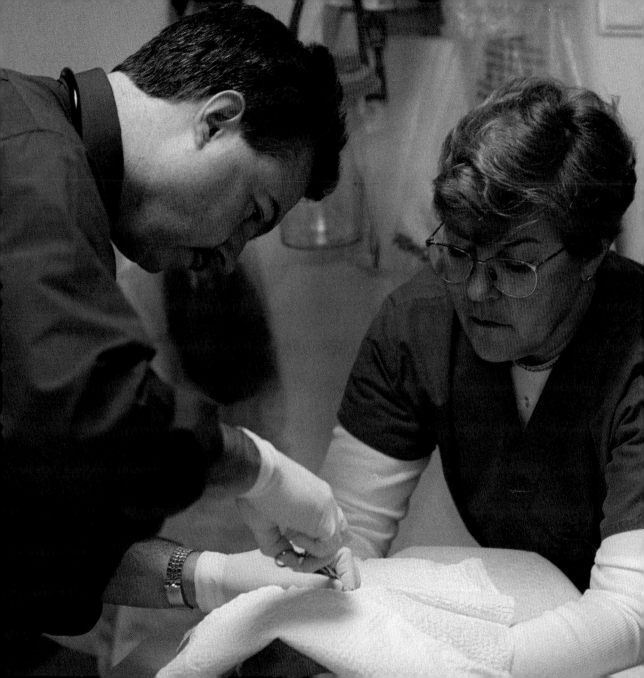

Getting Stitches

Sewing up skin sounds painful, but it isn't. Actually, you might not even feel the doctor putting in the stitches. The doctor will give you a small shot of **anesthesia** to take away the pain. The anesthesia will **numb** the area around the cut. When the stitches are in place, the doctor will cover them with a bandage. The bandage will help keep your stitches clean. Later, when you take the bandage off, you will see a neat row of black stitches.

◀ *A specially trained doctor will carefully put in your stitches.*

Feeling Scared

Getting stitches might sound scary! It's okay if you feel nervous about getting stitches. The idea of getting stitches can make kids or adults worry. Some people are afraid of the hospital or their doctor's office. It's good to remember, though, that hospitals and doctors make people feel better. It's also good to remember that many people get stitches. If you have to get stitches, it might help to talk to someone who has gotten stitches. He or she can help you feel less scared.

Ask for help if you feel scared. ▶

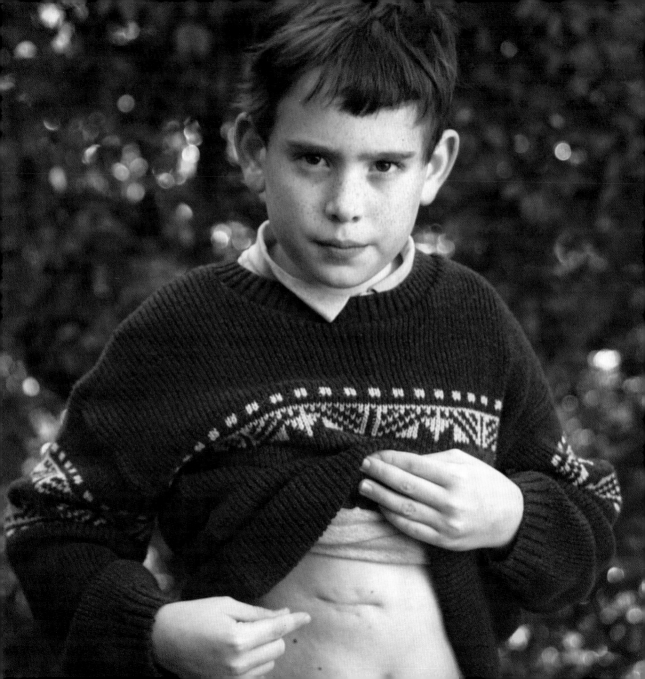

Reasons People Get Stitches

Stitches are used to close a big cut in the skin. You may need stitches if you have an accident and hurt yourself. People who go to the hospital to have surgery also may need stitches. When a person has an operation, the doctor cuts open the skin to take something out or fix something inside the body. That cut is sealed after the operation. Some cuts are closed with stitches. Some cuts are closed with special staples that are used in the hospital.

◀ *A scar on someone's tummy is often the result of an operation.*

Taking Care of Your Stitches

It is important to take care of your stitches so your cut will heal. You should keep your stitches clean. Do not touch, pull, or play with your stitches. You never should try to take out your own stitches! You also should keep your stitches covered with a loose bandage. If you put on a clean bandage every day, your cut will not get infected. Change your bandage if it gets wet or dirty. Treat the area where you have just had stitches with care so that you will not hurt it.

A parent or a friend can help you keep your ▶
stitches clean if they are hard for you to reach.

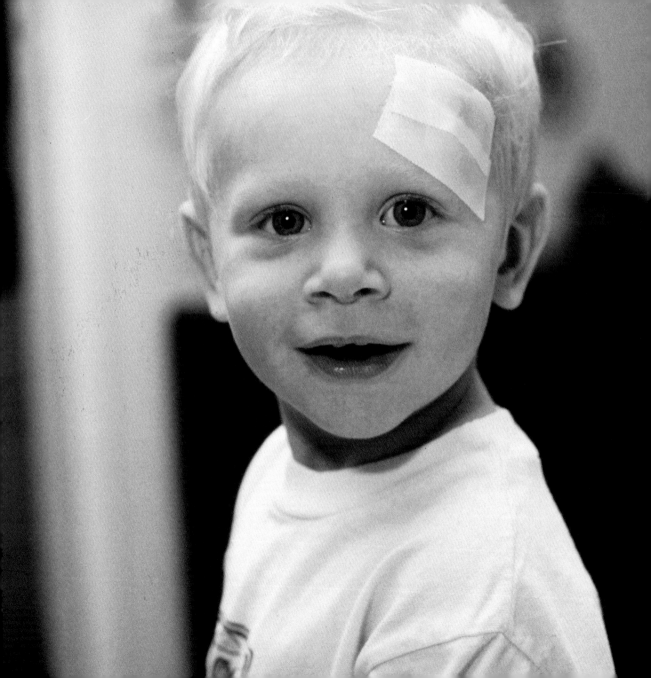

Getting Stitches Taken Out

When your cut has healed, you need to have your stitches taken out. Your doctor will do this for you. You never should take your stitches out by yourself. The doctor will cut each stitch with small scissors. Then the thread is gently pulled out of your skin. This will feel a little strange, but it does not hurt. Some stitches, such as those used in your mouth or inside your body, are made to **dissolve** when the cut has healed. Even though these stitches dissolve, you still need to visit the doctor for a checkup.

◀ *It is a good idea to put a bandage on your stitches to keep them clean.*

Getting Help When You Need Stitches

When you need to have stitches put in or taken out, ask someone you love to come with you. Perhaps your mom, dad, grandparent, or friend can help you. When you have someone you love nearby, you will feel less alone and less scared. Maybe you want someone to hold your hand. Maybe you could use help keeping your stitches clean. It is a good idea to have someone around to help you before, during, and after you get your stitches.

Glossary

anesthesia (a-nus-THEE-zhuh) Medicine to make feeling or pain
go away.

dissolve (dih-ZAHLV) To melt or fade away.

infected (in-FEK-tid) Having germs that cause disease.

numb (NUM) To cause to have no feeling or pain.

scar (SKAR) A mark left after broken skin has healed.

stitches (STICH-ez) The thread left in the skin after a needle is
passed in and out to close a cut.

Index

A
accident, 17
anesthesia, 13

B
bandage, 13, 18

D
dissolve, 21
doctor(s), 13, 14, 17, 21

H
heal(ed), 9, 10, 18, 21
hospital, 14, 17

I
infected, 9, 18

N
needle, 6
numb, 13

O
operation, 17

S
scar, 10
scared, 14, 22
sewn, 6
staples, 17

T
thread, 6, 21